05/18

3

D0983431

MAPLE SYRUP

40+ RECIPES FROM CHEFS ACROSS THE COUNTRY
THAT CELEBRATE THIS CANADIAN TREAT

ELAINE ELLIOT

FORMAC PUBLISHING COMPANY LIMITED
HALIFAX

Formac Publishing Company Limited recognizes the support of the Province of Nova Scotia through the Department of Communities, Culture and Heritage. We are pleased to work in partnership with the Culture Division to develop and promote our culture resources for all Nova Scotians. We acknowledge the financial support of the Government of Canada through the Canada Book Fund for our publishing activities. We acknowledge the support of the Canada Council for the Arts which last year invested $24.3 million in writing and publishing throughout Canada.

Cover design: Meghan Collins
Cover images: Shutterstock

Library and Archives Canada Cataloguing in Publication

Elliot, Elaine, 1939-, author
    Maple syrup : 40+ recipes from chefs across the country that celebrate this Canadian treat / Elaine Elliot. -- 2nd edition.

Includes index.
ISBN 978-1-4595-0444-8 (hardback)

    1. Cooking (Maple sugar and syrup). 2. Maple syrup. 3. Cookbooks. I. Title.

TX767.M3E445 2016   641.6'364   C2016-901808-3

Formac Publishing Company Limited
5502 Atlantic Street
Halifax, Nova Scotia, Canada
B3H 1G4
www.formac.ca

Printed and bound in China.

CONTENTS

INTRODUCTION

How did anyone ever discover that the sap from a tree, a particular tree, a maple tree in fact, could be collected (at a very particular time of year) and rendered into one of the sweetest treats in the land? Legends abound but it is clear that it was aboriginal First Nations who made this remarkable contribution to the culinary wealth of Eastern Canada. Maple syrup is a natural sweetener offering a unique flavour and many health benefits. Native people used it as a sweetener and a medicine, and early settlers used it as a substitute for sugar. Pancakes and maple syrup have been a famous gastronomic partnership for generations. In recent years maple syrup has become a refined and sophisticated ingredient in home cooking and gourmet cuisine. In this book chefs and innkeepers from across Canada share maple recipes in just about every category from savouries to sweets.

There are some half-dozen species of the maple tree (genus *Acer*) native to Canada, and several introduced varieties. The range of the maple in North America extends from Newfoundland and the Maritime provinces, through southern Quebec and Ontario to southeastern Manitoba, and south into the United States as far as Georgia. The maple has long been valued for its wood, its foliage and its sap.

The maple is a tree for all seasons. In summer it provides a dense canopy of shade. Its winter tracery on snow inspires artists and its wood keeps the home fires burning. The spectacle of brilliant wine, scarlet, amber and yellow maple foliage is an autumn delight. But in spring the maple outperforms all other trees. In springtime maple trees create the sweet sap from which maple sugar and syrup are made.

Sap flows to some degree in all species of maple but there are just four species that produce the quantity and quality of sap necessary for the production of maple syrup.

Sugar maple (*Acer saccharum*), also commonly called rock maple or hard maple, grows to around 30 metres tall and 60 to 90 centimetres in diameter and lives for two to three hundred years. Its leaves, dark green with lighter green undersides,

have three to five lobes or points separated by rounded indentations. Sugar maple occurs naturally throughout most of southeastern Canada and the northeastern United States.

The wood of the sugar maple is hard, strong and beautiful. It is used for flooring, furniture and sporting equipment as well as for fine woodworking and musical instruments. It also makes excellent firewood. Because of its high sugar content, the sugar maple is the mainstay of Eastern Canada's maple syrup and sugar industry.

Red maple (*Acer rubrum*), symbol of Canada and basis for our flag, is more abundant in Atlantic Canada than the sugar maple but is not as large or as hard. Its leaf shape is similar to the sugar maple but the lobes are serrated and the valleys between the lobes are sharp Vs. The green leaves are silverish on the underside and become strikingly scarlet in the autumn. Red maple is often used as an ornamental. It has essentially the same uses as the sugar maple, including maple syrup production, though it yields less sap. The sap flow season is shorter because red maple begins its growth earlier in spring than sugar maple. The red maple ranges from Newfoundland to

Manitoba in Canada and in the United States as far south as Texas and east to Florida.

Black maple (*Acer nigrum*) rivals the sugar maple as a producer of sap. However, it has a much smaller range, most of which is in the northeastern United States. Within Canada black maple is found only in the southernmost tip of Quebec.

Silver maple (*Acer saccharinum*), a species introduced into Canada from the United States, should be mentioned although it is not significant in the commercial maple syrup industry. Silver maple is a rapidly growing but relatively short-lived maple found throughout much of the eastern United States and extreme southeastern Canada. Although it is often tapped, silver maple is not generally considered suitable for commercial production because of its low sugar content and shorter collecting season. Sap with low sugar content requires much more evaporation, which means that production is more costly.

A stand of maple trees from which sap is harvested is called a sugarbush. Many sugarbushes tap both red and sugar maples.

To make maple syrup, it is not enough to have the right trees. The right climate and weather conditions are also prerequisites. Fortunately, these conditions prevail in a large part of Eastern Canada. Sugaring at a commercial level occurs in Quebec, Ontario, New Brunswick and Nova Scotia.

Maple syrup production is a very time-sensitive affair. There is a small window of four to six weeks between late February and mid-April during which the sap runs. When daytime temperature rises above freezing and

nights dip below freezing for several days in succession, physiological changes occur in the maple, causing sap to flow. Ideal temperatures for sap flow are 5°C during the day and -4°C at night.

During the summer months, maples accumulate starch. When weather starts to warm up in spring, enzymes in the tree start to change the starch into sugar. Groundwater is absorbed by the roots and combines with that sugar. The resulting sap is 97.5 percent water. Alternate freezing and thawing changes the pressure inside the tree, causing the sap to flow. It travels up the trunk during the day and runs down again toward the root system at night. It is the up-and-down movement of the sap that allows some to flow through tap holes to be collected in buckets or plastic tubing.

Sap collected early in the season makes light-coloured syrup while end-of-season sap results in dark syrup called "buddy sap" with a very strong flavour and odour. As maples begin their growth period, chemical changes in the sap make it unsuitable for syrup production. The season ends when nights stay above freezing and daytime temperatures warm to above 10°C, at which time trees begin to bud.

The whole process from sap collection to finished product must be accomplished quickly. Sap that is stored will begin to ferment within one to three days depending on temperatures.

The sap, when collected, is an almost tasteless, slightly sweetish, colourless liquid. What alchemy turns this unprepossessing substance into the amber nectar called maple syrup?

Maple syrup production is essentially a process of sap collection and evaporation. As sap is boiled, it becomes more concentrated and begins to

take on its distinctive maple flavour. It sounds simple enough, but it is, in fact, a very precise and time-consuming operation.

Native people showed early French settlers in Eastern Canada how to collect the sap by making a gash in the tree and placing a birch-bark or wooden trough at the base of the tree. The gash method was soon replaced by an auger hole in the trunk, into which a hollow tube or spile was inserted, and eventually metal spouts or spigots were introduced. The sap flowed easily into a metal pail that could now be hung from the tap. Plastic tubing and vacuum pumps, introduced in the 1960s, replaced the spigot and pail. The vacuum pump increases the flow of sap and the plastic tubes transport the sap directly to the sugarshack.

Buckets of sap were collected and either carried to the boiling site or emptied into a wooden barrel on a horse- or ox-drawn sledge for transport to the sugarshack. The twentieth century brought tractor-drawn vehicles with metal tanks to the maple woods.

The early settlers boiled the sap down in a cauldron over an open fire. Then rough lean-tos and later huts were constructed near the sugarbush to offer some protection to the syrup and the boiler. These evolved

into the sugarshacks of today where sap is boiled down to make maple syrup. Sugarshacks need to be well-ventilated to allow the moisture to dissipate.

The process of boiling down the sap is very slow because most of the water has to boil out of the sap before it is of the right consistency and sugar concentration. A round-bottomed cauldron was not very efficient for this purpose. In the 1800s the introduction of flat-bottomed pans reduced boiling time.

The evaporator, invented in 1860, was the most important factor in the evolution of sugaring as a modern industry. The evaporator has sectional dividers that allow cold sap to be let in at one end and finished sap to be drawn off at the other end. The time-consuming batch method gave way to continuous production. The evaporator cut down production time and produced a better product. Sap is fed into the evaporator units and kept at a constant level by a float. As the sap moves through the evaporator, it becomes more concentrated. The invention of the flue pan, which directs partially concentrated sap into the finishing pan, further improved the process.

The syrup is drawn off, tested and graded before being passed through a filter for bottling. Raw syrup contains suspended particles called sugar sand. In earlier days, these particles were allowed to settle in bulk containers before bottling. Modern filtration through cloth or paper membranes produces crystal-clear syrup.

Maple syrup is boiled down further to make maple cream or butter, maple candy and maple sugar. Maple cream, which is sold in plastic tubs, is a soft spread made by heating finished maple syrup to 113°C, then cooling it to 21°C and whipping to incorporate air into the thickened mass. Maple candy,

which is made by heating finished maple syrup to a temperature of 113°C and then cooling to 68°C and pouring into candy moulds, is another maple delight. Maple sugar is made by continuing to boil down the syrup until almost all liquid has evaporated. The sugar is about twice as sweet as granulated sugar and imparts a wonderful maple flavour when used to sweeten a drink or in baking.

Maple syrup is traditionally boiled over a hardwood fire, but today natural or bottled gas is more frequently used for better heat control. Heat must be carefully regulated to optimize evaporation without scorching the syrup or jeopardizing its colour or quality.

Farmers of earlier times harvested their trees each season, providing a sweetener for their own use and allowing them to sell or barter the surplus to those without a tree stand. Sugaring was an extension of the farming calendar, allowing a small cash crop in the spring before the first fields could be planted.

What began as a supplemental farm operation or a small hobby enterprise has become, with the introduction of modern equipment and procedures, an industry in its own right. Sound sugarbush management, better sanitation in the sugarbush operation and improved equipment in the sugarshack have improved the quality and marketability of the product. Maple products, once only available at the source and in season, are now available in supermarkets and specialty shops year-round.

A mature maple tree will yield about 30 to 40 litres of sap during the four- to six-week season. This will condense into only 1 litre of syrup. Thus to produce a marketable quantity of syrup, thousands of trees must be tapped. In order to sustain a tree stand, harvesters must not over-tax their trees. A well-cared-for

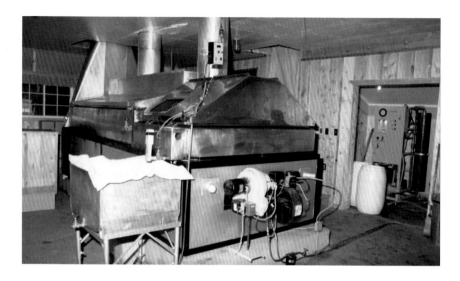

stand will produce sap for 200 years. It takes about 30 to 40 years for a maple to grow to a size suitable for tapping, and a tree with a diameter of 25 to 35 centimetres (measured at chest height) can accommodate only one tap hole. Larger trees, with a girth of 50 to 60 centimetres, may accommodate up to 3 tap holes.

Strict regulations govern the industry. Maple syrup can be legally offered for sale when its density has reached at least 66 percent sugar or, to use the technical term, 66° on the Brix scale. To obtain this minimum density of 66° the syrup must be boiled until it reaches a temperature 3.94°C above the boiling point of water. Hydrometers and thermometers calculate sugar density and indicate when the syrup is finished. Syrup with higher densities of 66.5° to 67.5° on the Brix scale produce a more pronounced maple flavour and a better palatability because of an increased viscosity. These densities are reached at temperatures of 4.06°C to 4.28°C above the boiling point of water.

The Canadian Food Inspection Agency monitors the safety and quality of maple syrup and ensures that producers meet federal standards. A grading system ensures standardization of the product for colour and flavour. There are three grades and five classes of colour: Canada No. 1 – extra light, light and medium are considered premium quality and constitute 25–30 percent each of total production. Canada No. 2 – amber is darker in colour and has a stronger flavour. It accounts for 10 percent. Purists feel that the stronger-flavoured syrups are ideal for cooking and baking. Canada No. 3 – dark (2 percent) has a hearty flavour and is deemed very suitable for cooking.

There are many table syrups, pancake syrups and maple-flavoured syrups

on the market but these are not maple products. "Pure Maple Syrup" on the label guarantees a genuine maple product. The grades and colour class of the syrup will also be on the label.

Pure maple syrup keeps in the freezer at -18°C for over a year and does not solidify. Unopened containers can be stored in a cool, dry place for up to six months. Opened containers must be stored, tightly covered, in a refrigerator.

It's hard to believe that something this sweet and tasty is also good for you, but it's true. One hundred percent pure maple syrup contains no preservatives, artificial colours or flavourings. It is a natural sweetener, full of natural sugars and nutrients. It has fewer calories and a higher concentration of minerals than other sweeteners. A 50 mL serving provides approximately 167 calories, 43 g of sugar, 117 mg of potassium, 7 mg of sodium and no fat. It provides 6 percent of the recommended daily intake of calcium and thiamine and 2 percent of magnesium and riboflavin. Maple syrup is an excellent source of manganese and a good source of zinc. Maple syrup offers benefits to the immune system and heart health.

The complexion of the sugaring operation has changed through the years. Small farms have gone out of business. Larger farms have become more specialized. Many maple syrup producers feature open-house weekends during the sugaring season, some offering pancake feasts or other culinary treats made with this delectable syrup. An excursion to a sugar camp to taste sugar on snow has been (in some families) a springtime tradition for generations.

Maple syrup production is concentrated in Eastern North America. Canada produces about 85 percent of the world's maple syrup, exporting more than

29,000 tonnes to over 30 countries worldwide. The industry is worth around $145 million annually. There are more than 10,000 maple syrup producers in Canada. The province of Quebec produces about 85 percent of Canada's maple syrup, with the remainder supplied by Ontario, New Brunswick and Nova Scotia.

The maple syrup industry in Canada today is solid, and as stable as its nature allows. The industry has not expanded in recent years nor has it experienced an appreciable decline. Natural calamities cause more damage than dieback and insects. A recent potential threat posed by the gypsy moth seems to have been overcome.

Maple trees, and therefore the maple syrup industry, are susceptible to the vagaries of nature. Trees will yield less sap in warmer winters. Likewise, times of drought will adversely affect sap production. It is possible to have several bad years in a row followed by a run of excellent productivity. Severe windstorms such as Hurricane Juan, which cut a swath through Nova Scotia in 2003, uproot trees and break limbs, causing serious setbacks to producers. Probably the most devastating natural disaster to the industry is an ice storm. In 1998 a severe ice storm paralyzed Quebec and decimated the maple woods, setting production back for several years. Fortunately, the maple is a very resilient species. It is wonderfully long-lived and generally quite healthy. It has the ability to recover from natural disasters. In maple woods, there is constant natural regeneration. Maple seedlings grow in the shade provided by the big crowns of mature trees. As older trees die off (this can take up to 400 years) young trees are ready to fill the gaps.

More significant to the ongoing health and growth of the industry is the

declining workforce. Maple syrup operations were traditionally passed down through generations. Today, as with agriculture generally, fewer young people want to stay on the farm. The work is hard; the outcome unpredictable. With the possibility of five or six years of poor yield, the reluctance to put in the sweat equity and take the risk is understandable.

Some small producers have ensured the viability of their operation and an independent livelihood by expanding their sugaring operation into a year-round tourism business. They continue the springtime tradition of making maple syrup over an evaporator fired with mountain hardwood and produce maple products in an ecologically sound manner. Draft horse power may be employed on the farm, and sleigh rides offered in winter. Visitors learn about the history and craft of maple sugaring and maple syrup, hike through the sugar maples to see the pipelines and sample sugar on snow. Pancake meals are served, perhaps in a log pancake house, and a variety of maple products are offered for sale.

Times have changed from the Quebec sugaring scenes immortalized in the paintings of Cornelius Krieghoff. But the time-honoured tradition of harvesting maple sap in the springtime to produce maple syrup and sugar continues. The taste is the same but the product is better and more popular than ever. Gourmet chefs and home cooks are experimenting with maple flavours in a wide variety of dishes—meat and fish, salads and dressings, vegetables and legumes, and of course, desserts and drinks. So, open your mind and palate to some wonderful flavours and enjoy!

Peerless Cranberry Maple Sugar Scones, p.18

BREAKFAST & BRUNCH

If you think maple syrup is simply a pancake topper, think again! In this section there are a number of breakfast or brunch options, all using pure maple syrup.

PEERLESS CRANBERRY MAPLE SUGAR SCONES

Wickwire House Bed and Breakfast, Kentville, NS

Maple sugar, which is about twice as sweet as white sugar, is made by continuing to boil down the maple sap until the liquid has almost completely evaporated. At Wickwire House, the scones are served with jam or English Double Devon Cream.

1½ cups (375 mL) all-purpose flour
¼ cup (60 mL) maple sugar
1 tsp (5 mL) baking powder
¼ tsp (1 mL) salt
¼ tsp (1 mL) baking soda
⅓ cup (75 mL) dried cranberries
grated zest of 1 orange
⅓ cup (75 mL) butter
½ cup (125 mL) sour cream
1–2 tbsp (15–30 mL) maple sugar (second amount)

Preheat oven to 400°F (200°C). In a mixing bowl combine flour, maple sugar, baking powder, salt and baking soda. Stir in dried cranberries and orange zest. Cut in butter until mixture resembles coarse crumbs; stir in sour cream. Shape dough into a ball and pat into an 8 inch (20 cm) round on a lightly greased cookie sheet. Cut dough into eight wedges and sprinkle with additional maple sugar. Bake 18 to 20 minutes or until lightly browned.

Yields 8 wedges

WELLINGTON COURT COFFEE

Wellington Court Restaurant, St. Catherines, ON

Chef Erik Peacock of Wellington Court Restaurant likes to serve his coffee tableside in a bodum-style coffee maker. He generously shares his secret ingredient with us.

1 bodum-style carafe of coffee
pure maple syrup, to taste
milk, to foam for garnish

Prepare coffee and pour. Sweeten coffee with a teaspoon of maple syrup or to taste. Using a cappuccino frother, foam milk. Garnish cup with a dollop of foamed milk. How simple, how sweet!

ORANGE CARDAMOM FRENCH TOAST

Copper Chimney Indian Grill and Bar, Vancouver, BC

This variation of your mother's French toast will sweep you off your feet. Its citrus flavour with just a hint of exotic cardamom is simply the best!

8 eggs
¾ cup (175 mL) half-and-half (10% m.f.)
3 tbsp (45 mL) grated orange zest
¾ cup (175 mL) orange juice
2 tbsp (30 mL) Grand Marnier liqueur
1½ tsp (7 mL) ground cardamom
1 loaf white country bread or fruit bread, thinly sliced
2–3 tbsp (30–45 mL) butter
fresh seasonal berries
icing sugar
pure maple syrup, warmed

Beat together eggs, cream, orange zest, orange juice and liqueur in a bowl. Stir in cardamom and let stand for 1 hour.

Soak bread slices in egg mixture, turning once. In a skillet, heat 1 tbsp (15 mL) butter over medium heat; fry bread slices for 2 to 3 minutes per side or until golden and centre is cooked. Repeat for remaining slices, adding more butter to skillet as necessary.

To serve, top French toast with berries, a dusting of icing sugar and warm maple syrup.

Serves 4–6

PANCAKES WITH FRENCH VANILLA YOGURT, APPLES AND RAISINS

This recipe makes four large pancakes—it is beautiful in its presentation and equally delicious.

1½ cups (375 mL) all-purpose flour
1 tbsp (15 mL) baking powder
pinch of salt
1½ cups (375 mL) milk
2 eggs
2 tbsp (30 mL) vegetable oil
butter, for cooking pancakes
2 large apples, peeled, cored and thinly sliced
½ cup (125 mL) raisins
½ cup (125 mL) French vanilla yogurt
icing sugar, as garnish
pure maple syrup

Combine flour, baking powder and salt in a large bowl. In a separate bowl whisk together the milk, eggs and vegetable oil. Slowly incorporate milk mixture into flour mixture, stirring only until combined.

Grease a large skillet with butter and heat to 400°F (200°C). Pour ¼ of the batter into pan and cook until small bubbles appear. Flip pancake and cook other side.

Place prepared apple slices and raisins in a microwave-safe dish and process on high until apples are soft, about 1 minute. Keep warm.

To serve, fill middle of pancake with ¼ of the apple/raisin mixture and 2 tbsp (30 mL) yogurt. Fold pancake in half, omelette-style, and serve with a sprinkle of icing sugar, maple syrup and additional raisins. Repeat.

Serves 4

BLUEBERRY WAFFLES WITH MAPLE SYRUP

Luscious, browned waffles are a nice variation for Sunday brunch. Treat yourself to a warm waffle covered with butter and your favourite brand of maple syrup.

1½ cups (375 mL) all-purpose flour
2 tbsp (30 mL) granulated sugar
½ tsp (2 mL) salt
½ tsp (2 mL) baking soda
1 tsp (5 mL) baking powder
1½ cups (375 mL) buttermilk
2 eggs, beaten
¼ cup (60 mL) vegetable oil or melted butter
½ cup (125 mL) blueberries, washed and dried
½ cup (125 mL) pure maple syrup, warmed

Combine flour, sugar, salt, baking soda and baking powder in a large bowl. In another bowl, whisk together buttermilk, eggs and oil. Add liquid to dry ingredients, stirring only until smooth.

Preheat waffle iron according to manufacturer's directions. Pour batter onto hot waffle iron and sprinkle with 1 tbsp (15 mL) blueberries. Bake until steaming stops and waffle is golden. Serve immediately with warmed maple syrup.

Serves 4

FRENCH TOAST STUFFED WITH MAPLE-GLAZED APPLES

While the chef's recipe calls for apples, she suggests that fresh peaches may be sutstituted and are equally delicious.

6–8 slices fresh homemade bread, sliced 2 inches (5 cm) thick
½ cup (125 mL) light cream
4 eggs, beaten
½ cup (125 mL) butter
¼ cup (60 mL) pecans
2 tart apples, pared and cut in small slices
¼ tsp (1 mL) cinnamon
¼ cup (60 mL) pure maple syrup
freshly ground nutmeg
2 tbsp (30 mL) butter (second amount)

Preheat oven to 150°F (65°C). Cut a pocket almost all the way through each slice of bread; set aside. In a bowl, combine cream and eggs.

Melt butter in a large skillet; stir in pecans, apple slices, cinnamon, maple syrup and a generous grating of fresh nutmeg. Bring to a simmer and cook, stirring frequently, until apples are barely tender. Remove from heat.

In a large skillet, over medium heat, melt second amount of butter. Dip one slice of bread at a time in egg mixture, pressing down to allow eggs to soak through. Lift out, allowing excess egg mixture to drip back into the bowl. Fry the soaked bread until golden brown, on one side only, about 2 minutes. Carefully open pocket and spoon in a small amount of the pecan mixture. Flip bread and brown other side, repeating procedure and adding more butter if necessary. Keep toast warm in a 150°F (65°C) oven . Serve with additional maple syrup and seasonal fruit.

Serves 4–6

WICKWIRE HOUSE MAPLE PECAN BANANA PANCAKES

Wickwire House Bed and Breakfast, Kentville, NS

The innkeeper roasts the pecans to enhance their flavour. Toast the pecans by sprinkling them on a cookie sheet and baking in a moderate oven for 2 to 3 minutes. Cool on a wire rack for 20 minutes before serving.

2 extra large eggs
2 cups (500 mL) buttermilk
2 cups (500 mL) mashed bananas
¼ cup (60 mL) maple syrup
¼ cup (60 mL) vegetable oil
2¼ cups (560 mL) all-purpose flour
1 tbsp (15 mL) baking powder
1 tsp (5 mL) baking soda
¼ tsp (1 mL) salt
1 cup (250 mL) chopped pecans, toasted
3 medium bananas, sliced
3 cups (750 mL) fresh strawberry halves
pure maple syrup

Beat eggs in a large bowl until fluffy, approximately 2 minutes. Combine buttermilk, mashed bananas, ¼ cup (60 mL) maple syrup and vegetable oil with egg mixture and set aside. In a separate bowl, combine flour, baking powder, baking soda, salt and pecans. Add liquid ingredients, stirring only until just blended.

Heat a non-stick griddle to 375°F (190°C), greasing lightly as necessary. Pour approximately ¼ cup (60 mL) batter per pancake onto griddle and cook until puffed and dry around the edges, then turn over and cook until golden brown. Serve pancakes with sliced bananas and strawberry halves; drizzle with additional maple syrup.

Yields twenty-four 4 inch (10 cm) pancakes

MAPLE SYRUP GINGERBREAD

Liscombe Lodge, Liscomb Mills, NS

Savour this cake warm from the oven over a final cup of coffee. This old-time favourite takes on a new flavour with the addition of maple syrup.

1⅓ cups (325 mL) all-purpose flour
1 tsp (5 mL) baking powder
1 tsp (5 mL) ginger
½ tsp (2 mL) baking soda
½ tsp (2 mL) salt
¾ cup (175 mL) pure maple syrup
½ cup (125 mL) vegetable oil
1 egg, beaten
⅓ cup (75 mL) warm water

Preheat oven to 375°F (190°C) and butter a 9 inch (23 cm) round cake pan.

Mix together the dry ingredients in a large bowl. In a separate bowl, combine maple syrup, oil and egg, beating until smooth; blend in warm water. Make a well in the dry ingredients and add the syrup mixture, stirring until flour mixture is moistened. Pour into prepared pan and bake 30 minutes or until cake springs back in the centre when lightly touched.

Serves 6–8

MAPLE APPLE COFFEE CAKE

Inn on the Lake, Waverley, NS

This moist cake combines the wonderful flavours of tart Nova Scotia apples and pure maple syrup, making it an ideal accompaniment to your morning coffee.

½ cup (125 mL) butter, softened
3 eggs
½ cup (125 mL) pure maple syrup
2 tsp (10 mL) vanilla
2 cups (500 mL) all-purpose flour
2 tsp (10 mL) baking powder
⅛ tsp (0.5 mL) salt
1 tsp (5 mL) cinnamon
¼ tsp (1 mL) nutmeg

TOPPING:

3 large tart apples, peeled, cored and sliced
¼ tsp (1 mL) freshly ground nutmeg
4 tbsp (60 mL) granulated sugar
½ tsp (2 mL) cinnamon (second amount)
2 tbsp (30 mL) butter, melted

Preheat oven to 375°F (190°C) and butter a 9-inch (23 cm) round cake pan. Beat butter with an electric mixer until light and fluffy. Add eggs one at a time, beating well after each addition. Add maple syrup and vanilla and continue to beat until mixture is fully combined.

In a separate bowl, sift together flour, baking powder, salt, cinnamon and nutmeg. Fold dry ingredients into butter mixture and spoon the batter into the prepared pan.

Prepare topping by tossing apples with nutmeg, sugar, cinnamon and butter. Arrange decoratively on top of batter and bake 50 to 60 minutes until the apples are tender and a toothpick inserted in the centre of the cake comes out clean. Remove to a wire rack and allow to cool 10 minutes before removing from the pan. Serve warm, sliced in wedges.

Serves 8

GRILLED SABAYON FRUIT CREPES

Cobble House Bed and Breakfast, Cobble Hill, BC

You will undoubtedly serve this signature recipe from innkeepers Ingrid and Simon Vermegen again and again. They note that should fresh blueberries be unavailable, you may substitute drained frozen berries.

CREPES:

1 cup (250 mL) milk
1 egg
1 cup (250 mL) all-purpose flour
pinch of salt
vegetable oil for cooking crepes
Fruit Filling (recipe follows)
Maple Syrup Sabayon (recipe follows)
fresh raspberries, as garnish

Mix milk, egg, flour and salt together in a large bowl until no lumps remain. Heat a non-stick–coated frying pan on medium-high and add a little vegetable oil. Pour in ¼ of the batter and cook until golden brown. Flip crepe and brown other side. Remove crepe from pan and keep warm. Repeat.

Preheat broiler to 375°F (190°C). Place a crepe on each of four oven-proof plates. Divide Fruit Filling between the crepes and fold over. Spoon a little Maple Syrup Sabayon over crepes and place under the broiler to lightly brown the sauce. Watch carefully—this happens quite quickly. Serve warm from the oven, garnished with fresh raspberries.

FRUIT FILLING:

½ cup (125 mL) orange juice
2 tsp (10 mL) cornstarch
2 medium apples, peeled, cored and cubed
2 oranges, peeled and chopped
zest of 1 lemon
1 cup (250 mL) fresh blueberries

Stir cornstarch into orange juice and combine in a saucepan with apples, oranges and lemon zest; bring to a full boil. Immediately reduce heat and simmer until thickened. Remove from heat and fold in blueberries. Keep warm.

MAPLE SYRUP SABAYON:

¼ cup (60 mL) pure maple syrup
3 eggs
2 tsp (10 mL) brandy

Using a double boiler, combine maple syrup, eggs and brandy over simmering water. Beat mixture with a whisk until it is foamy and firm. Keep warm.

TINY SCOTTISH PANCAKES WITH BRANDIED MAPLE SYRUP

The Murray Manor Bed and Breakfast, Yarmouth, NS

The Murray Manor serves these tiny pancakes accompanied by pure maple syrup infused with a wee dram of brandy.

2 eggs
½ cup (125 mL) granulated sugar
1 tsp (5 mL) vanilla
1 cup (250 mL) milk
1½ cups (375 mL) all-purpose flour
1 tbsp (15 mL) baking powder
¼ tsp (1 mL) salt
1 tbsp (15 mL) butter, melted
½ cup (125 mL) blueberries
oil for browning, as necessary
¾ cup (175 mL) pure maple syrup
2 tbsp (30 mL) brandy

Preheat a griddle to 375°F (190°C). In a large mixing bowl, combine eggs, sugar and vanilla; add milk. In a separate bowl, sift together the flour, baking powder and salt. Add flour to egg mixture, mixing only until blended. Stir in melted butter and blueberries.

Lightly oil griddle and pour on approximately 1 tablespoon of batter for each pancake. As small bubbles appear on the top, turn and brown the other side. Combine pure maple syrup and brandy in a small pitcher and serve over pancakes.

Yields 20–24 small pancakes

Carriage House Inn Salad, p. 34

SALADS, SIDES & ACCOMPÁNIMENTS

Pure maple syrup—a gift from the gods! In this section you will find many recipes using the subtle taste of maple to infuse and flavour dishes.

CARRIAGE HOUSE INN SALAD

Carriage House Inn, Fredericton, NB

The innkeeper of Fredericton's Carriage House serves this dressing with torn spinach leaves and a choice of freshly shelled nuts.

1 clove garlic
2 green onions or several fresh parsley sprigs
½ tsp (2 mL) dried basil
3 tbsp (45 mL) pure maple syrup
¼ cup (60 mL) vinegar
1 cup (250 mL) canola or corn oil
prepared spinach leaves to serve 6
½ cup (125 mL) nuts (pine, almonds, walnuts or pecans)

Place garlic, onions or parsley, basil, maple syrup and vinegar in a blender and process on medium speed. Slowly add the oil in a thin, steady stream while processing until dressing has emulsified.

Place prepared spinach in a large salad bowl. Toss with nuts and drizzle with dressing. Store unused dressing in a tightly capped container in refrigerator up to 5 days.

Yields 1¼ cups (310 mL) salad dressing

OPEN SESAME SALMON WITH ZUCCHINI RIBBON SALAD

Smith Restaurant at Inn at the Forks, Winnipeg, MN

One of the most popular items on the menu, this salad makes a wonderful summer meal any time of day. At the restaurant, chef Barry Saunders uses a mandoline to slice his zucchini but notes that this can be accomplished using a sharp paring knife.

4 salmon fillets, 5 oz. (155 g) each
½ cup (125 mL) pure maple syrup
1 cup (250 mL) low-sodium soy sauce
2 tbsp (30 mL) grated fresh ginger
2 tbsp (30 mL) black and white sesame seeds, toasted
1 lime, cut in wedges
4 cilantro sprigs
Zucchini Ribbon Salad (recipe follows)

Rinse salmon fillets and pat dry. In a deep-sided dish, combine maple syrup, soy sauce and fresh ginger. Marinate fillets, refrigerated, at least 8 hours and up to 24 hours, turning several times.

Heat a non-stick skillet over medium heat and toast sesame seeds about 1 minute, shaking pan frequently. Remove seeds and set aside. Drain salmon and sear on both sides until nicely caramelised. Cook to desired doneness.

Divide Zucchini Ribbon Salad onto 4 serving plates. Top each salad with a salmon fillet and garnish with a sprinkling of sesame seeds, a lime wedge and a cilantro sprig.

Serves 4

ZUCCHINI RIBBON SALAD

2 small zucchini, about ¾ lb (375 g) total
½ small red onion, peeled and cut in thin strips
½ mango, peeled and cut in small dice
½ medium red pepper, seeded and cut in thin strips
fresh cilantro, roughly chopped, to taste
juice from 1 small lime
2 tbsp (30 mL) sesame oil
¼ cup (60 mL) sweet chilli sauce
sea salt, to taste

Using a mandoline, adjust the blades to approximately ⅛ inch (1 cm) thickness. Slice zucchini creating a ribbon or fettuccini shape until centre seeds are reached. Discard centre. Blanch zucchini ribbons in boiling salted water for 30 to 40 seconds or until al dente. Strain and cool in ice water. When cool, remove from ice water and lay on towel to dry.

In a bowl combine zucchini, onion, mango, red pepper and cilantro. In a separate bowl whisk together lime juice, sesame oil and sweet chilli sauce. Drizzle over zucchini and gently toss.

Serves 4

NOVA SCOTIA MAPLE SYRUP BAKED BEANS

Liscombe Lodge, Liscomb Mills, NS

At Liscombe Lodge, the chef serves his maple-infused baked beans with his breakfast menu. I think you will enjoy the delicate flavour of his rendition of baked beans.

1 lb. (500 g) dry white beans, rinsed and cleaned
6 cups (1.5 L) water
6 slices bacon, cut in 2 inch (5 cm) pieces
1 small onion, chopped
½ tsp (2 mL) dry mustard
1½ tsp (7 mL) salt
½ cup (125 mL) dark maple syrup
2 tbsp (30 mL) brown sugar
2 tbsp (30 mL) butter, softened

Bring the beans and water to a boil in a large saucepan and boil for 2 minutes. Remove from heat and let stand, covered, for an hour. Return to a boil, reduce heat and simmer, covered, for 40 minutes. Drain, reserving cooking liquid.

Place half of the bacon in a bean crock; add beans. In a separate bowl, combine the reserved cooking liquid, onion, dry mustard, salt and maple syrup. Pour over the beans and top with remaining bacon. Bake, covered, at 325°F (160°C) for approximately 3 hours. From time to time, check beans and add a small amount of water if they appear dry.

Cream together the brown sugar and butter. Sprinkle over the beans and bake, uncovered, an additional hour.

Serves 6–8

ROASTED BUTTERNUT SQUASH SOUP WITH MAPLE CREAM

Pyramid Lake Resort, Jasper, AB

Roasting the squash prior to making this soup intensifies its flavour. In testing this recipe, I first used heavy cream as called for by the chef, and the results were heavenly. I also tested the soup using 10% cream and found it a little less rich but equally delicious.

1 butternut squash, about 3 lb. (1.5 kg)
4 tbsp (60 mL) butter, softened
¼ cup (60 mL) pure maple syrup
1 tbsp (15 mL) vegetable oil
1 large carrot, peeled and diced
½ large white onion, diced
1 stalk celery, diced
4 cups (1 L) chicken stock
2 cups (500 mL) heavy cream (35% m.f.)
¼ cup (60 mL) pure maple syrup (second amount)
salt and white pepper, to taste

Preheat oven to 325°F (160°C). Peel squash and cut in half. Scoop out seeds and spread butter over squash. Place cut side up on a rimmed baking sheet and drizzle with ¼ cup (60 mL) maple syrup. Roast until tender, about 50 minutes.

Using a large saucepan, sauté carrot, onion and celery in oil until vegetables begin to take on colour. Cube baked squash and add to vegetables along with any caramelised butter and syrup found in the pan. Add chicken stock and bring to a boil. Reduce heat and simmer until all the vegetables are tender, about 30 minutes. Using a blender, purée soup in batches. In a separate bowl, combine cream and second amount of maple syrup. Return soup to a boil and stir in ¾ of the maple cream mixture, reserving the rest as a garnish. Season to taste with salt and white pepper. Serve in warm bowls drizzled with remaining maple cream.

Serves 8

WILD RICE AND MUSHROOM SOUP

The chef tells us sherry may be substituted for the maple syrup in this recipe, producing an equally delicious soup.

3 cups (750 mL) chicken broth
⅓ cup (75 mL) raw wild rice, rinsed and drained
½ cup (125 mL) thinly sliced green onions
1 cup (250 mL) light cream (18% m.f.)
2 tbsp (30 mL) all-purpose flour
1 tsp (5 mL) fresh thyme or ¼ tsp (1 mL) dried
freshly ground pepper to taste
½ cup (125 mL) sliced fresh mushrooms
1 tbsp (15 mL) pure maple syrup

In a large saucepan, combine broth and uncooked wild rice. Bring to a boil, reduce heat and simmer, covered, for 40 minutes. Stir in green onions and cook an additional 5 to 10 minutes until rice is tender. In a small bowl, whisk together cream, flour, thyme and pepper. Stir cream into soup mixture and add mushrooms. Cook, stirring frequently, until soup is thickened and bubbly. Stir in maple syrup and heat through.

Serves 4

WHISKEY AND PEACH MAPLE GLAZE

The Briars, Jackson's Point, ON

You might want to serve this sauce with a variety of meats, but the chef tells me that it is especially delicious spooned over oven-baked or barbecued chicken breasts.

2 fresh peaches, peeled, halved and sliced
3 tbsp (45 mL) clarified butter*
2 shallots, thinly sliced
pinch of coarsely cracked black peppercorns
¼ cup (60 mL) Canadian Club whiskey
¼ cup (60 mL) pure maple syrup
1½ tbsp (22 mL) good quality balsamic vinegar

Prepare peaches and set aside. Heat clarified butter over high temperature and quickly sauté shallots and peppercorns, stirring constantly. When shallots have reached a golden colour, approximately 4 minutes, briefly remove pot from burner; add whiskey and flambé**. Return to heat, add peach slices and sauté until peaches are slightly softened; stir in maple syrup and cook until mixture is reduced to a thick syrup, about 7 minutes. Remove from heat and stir in balsamic vinegar. Serve warm.

Yields 1–1 ¼ cups (250–310 mL) sauce

*Clarified or drawn butter is prepared by slowly melting unsalted butter, thus evaporating most of the water and allowing the milk solids to sink to the bottom of the pan, leaving a golden liquid on the surface. Skim foam from surface, then pour or spoon the clarified butter into a container. It will take 4 tbsp (60 mL) of unsalted butter to make 3 tbsp (45 mL) clarified butter.

** To flambé, remove pan from burner, sprinkle with whiskey and ignite, shaking pan until flames are extinguished.

CRANBERRY MAPLE CHUTNEY

Deerhurst Resort, Huntsville, ON

Located in the beautiful Muskoka region of Ontario, the chefs at Deerhurst Resort rely upon an abundant supply of fresh cranberries from the bogs of nearby Bala. They serve the chutney with chicken or wild game, or as an accompaniment to patés and fresh fruit.

1 lb. (500 g) cranberries, fresh or frozen
2 tbsp (30 mL) vegetable oil
⅓ cup (75 mL) white vinegar
1 small onion, diced
½ tsp (2 mL) cinnamon
½ tsp (2 mL) nutmeg
½ tsp (2 mL) dry mustard
1 orange, juice and zest
⅓ cup (75 mL) pure maple syrup

Rinse cranberries, discarding any that are blemished, and set aside. Heat oil over medium heat in a large saucepan and cook diced onion until transparent, about 3 minutes. Do not allow onion to brown. Deglaze pan with white vinegar. Stir in cranberries, cinnamon, nutmeg, dry mustard, and juice and zest of the orange. Bring to a simmer and cook approximately 5 minutes or until the first of the cranberries start to pop. Remove from burner and stir in maple syrup. Cool. Should the chutney become too thick when cool, adjust with additional orange juice or maple syrup.

Yields 3 cups (750 mL)

MAPLE-GLAZED ROOT VEGETABLES POT AU FEU

The Keefer Mansion, Thorold, ON

The chef notes that if double-smoked bacon is unavailable, regular bacon may be used. He offers this assortment of root vegetables as a guide and suggests you choose your vegetables according to your family preferences. Whatever you choose, the aroma permeating throughout your kitchen will make this recipe a crowd-pleaser.

3 oz. (90 g) double-smoked bacon, cut into small pieces
5 shallots, finely diced
2 tbsp (30 mL) grapeseed oil
3 large carrots, peeled and diagonally sliced
3 large parsnips, peeled and diagonally sliced
2 cups (500 mL) pearl onions, peeled (mixed colours if possible)
3 small turnips, peeled and cut in wedges
1 rutabaga, peeled and cut in large dice
2 heads garlic, separated and peeled
½ cup (125 mL) white wine
1 bunch thyme
3 fresh sage leaves
¼ cup (60 mL) pure maple syrup
2 tbsp (30 mL) butter
salt and freshly ground pepper, to taste

Cook bacon and shallots with oil in a large ovenproof saucepan over medium heat until bacon is brown and shallots are translucent. Add all other vegetables and stir until evenly browned. Deglaze pan with wine and reduce until almost dry.

Add thyme to pan; cover and bake in a 350°F (180°C) oven for 15 minutes. While vegetables are baking bring maple syrup and butter to a boil then remove from heat. Stir into vegetables and bake an additional 10 minutes. Place sage leaves on top of vegetables; cover pan and return to oven for 10 minutes. Check for tenderness, and cook in increments of 5 minutes until vegetables are fork-tender. Remove herbs and season to taste with salt and freshly ground pepper.

Serves 6

CURRIED PINEAPPLE AND GINGER CHUTNEY

Keltic Lodge Resort and Spa, Ingonish Beach, NS

This gem of a condiment encompasses chunks of red and green bell peppers, fresh pineapple and onion in a gingered curry sauce. Try this as an accompaniment to a cheese tray, or with roasted chicken or pork!

2 tbsp (30 mL) canola oil
½ red bell pepper, cut into ½ inch (1.5 cm) squares
½ green bell pepper, cut into ½ inch (1.5 cm) squares
1½ red onions, peeled and cut into ½ inch (1.5 cm) wedges
2 tbsp (30 mL) minced fresh ginger
1½ tbsp (22 mL) minced fresh garlic
½ tbsp (7 mL) minced red or green chili pepper of choice
1½ tbsp (22 mL) curry powder
½ large pineapple, peeled, cored and cut into ½ inch (1.5 cm) chunks
¼ cup (60 mL) raisins
¾ cup (175 mL) white vinegar
¼ cup (60 mL) orange or pineapple juice
½ cup (125 mL) pure maple syrup
salt and freshly ground black pepper, to taste

In a large saucepan, heat oil over medium-high heat until hot but not smoking. Add bell peppers and onion and sauté, stirring constantly, until onion becomes translucent, about 5 to 6 minutes.

Add ginger, garlic, chili pepper and curry powder and sauté 1 minute. Add pineapple, raisins, vinegar, juice and maple syrup and bring to a boil. Reduce heat to low and simmer 10 to 15 minutes, stirring occasionally or until liquids have thickened slightly. Season with salt and freshly ground black pepper, remove from heat and cool to room temperature. Store chutney, covered and refrigerated, up to 10 days.

Yields 4 cups (1 L)

Lake Brome Duckling Braised in Maple Syrup Sauce, p. 60

ENTRÉES

The subtle flavour of maple syrup marries beautifully with poultry, pork and seafood. Chefs across the country are experimenting with its use. How innovative and how Canadian!

SUSUR LEE'S BARBECUED PORK TENDERLOIN

Susur Restaurant, Toronto, ON

The flavours in this recipe develop during the time allotted for marinating the meat, so you must begin to prepare this dish a day or two in advance of serving. Tenderloins are considered the most prized cut of pork, and Chef Susur Lee serves his barbecued tenderloins elegantly fanned on a plate accompanied by a succulent maple-infused sauce.

2 pork tenderloins, 12 oz. (375 g) each
1 medium rib celery, finely chopped
1 medium carrot, finely chopped
1 medium onion, finely chopped
1 tbsp (15 mL) minced fresh ginger
zest and juice of 1 small orange
⅔ cup (150 mL) rice cooking wine or
  dry sherry
⅓ cup (75 mL) soy sauce
⅓ cup (75 mL) pure maple syrup
2 tbsp (30 mL) dark sesame oil, divided

Trim tenderloins of silver skin and any excess fat; rinse and pat dry. In a shallow glass baking, dish combine celery, carrot, onion, ginger, orange zest and juice, wine, soy sauce and maple syrup. Add 1 tbsp (15 mL) of the sesame oil and stir to combine.

Add prepared tenderloins, turning to coat. Cover and let marinate in the refrigerator for 24 to 48 hours, turning occasionally.

Preheat the grill to medium-high. Remove tenderloins from the marinade and blot dry with paper towels. Strain the marinade into a small saucepan and bring to a boil over medium-high heat. Boil the marinade until slightly thickened and syrupy, about 10 minutes. Keep warm and set aside.

When ready to grill, brush the tenderloins with the remaining 1 tbsp (15 mL) sesame oil. Arrange the tenderloins on the hot grate; grill, turning with tongs, until the pork begins to brown, about 10 minutes. Transfer ¼ cup (60 mL) of cooked marinade to a small bowl and brush on pork. Continue to grill, turning and basting occasionally, an additional 6 to 10 minutes. When tested with an instant-read meat thermometer, the internal temperature should read 160°F (70°C). Transfer tenderloins to a cutting board and let rest 5 minutes. To serve, cut on the diagonal into ½ inch (1 cm) slices and fan on plates. Serve with reserved marinade.

Serves 4

FRESH THYME AND MAPLE SAUCE WITH ROCK CORNISH HENS

The Briars, Jackson's Point, ON

The chef at The Briars developed this recipe to serve with wild rice-stuffed cornish hens.

FRESH THYME AND MAPLE SAUCE:

¾ cup (175 mL) butter, melted
1 tbsp (15 mL) fresh thyme, chopped
1 cup (250 mL) pure maple syrup
½ cup (125 mL) Dijon mustard

In a saucepan over low heat, combine butter and chopped thyme and cook about 5 minutes. Add maple syrup and mustard; blend well. Set aside half the sauce to serve warm in a gravy boat with the Cornish hens.

Yields 2 cups (500 mL) sauce

ROCK CORNISH HENS (AUTHOR'S RECIPE):

6½ oz. (180 g) package wild rice
    stuffing mix
4 Rock Cornish hens, 1 lb. (500 g) each
salt and pepper
2 tbsp (30 mL) melted butter
1 cup (250 mL) Fresh Thyme and
    Maple Sauce

Following package directions, prepare wild rice stuffing mix and set aside to cool to room temperature.

Preheat oven to 350°F (180°C). Rinse Cornish hens under cold running water and pat dry. Gently stuff hens with stuffing and truss or skewer them shut. Season with a sprinkling of salt and pepper. Place hens in a shallow baking pan, brush with melted butter and bake 45 minutes. Remove from oven and baste with Fresh Thyme and Maple Sauce. Return to oven and continue to bake, basting frequently, until hens are browned and done, approximately 30 to 45 minutes longer. Remove to a serving platter and tent with foil. Serve accompanied by warm Fresh Thyme and Maple Sauce.

Serves 4

CITRUS AND MAPLE GLAZED SALMON FILLETS

*Our great Canadian maple syrup, when combined with fresh citrus juices,
makes a wonderful glaze for salmon.*

¼ cup (60 mL) olive oil
juice of 1 lemon
1 tbsp (15 mL) chili powder
½ tbsp (7 mL) minced fresh gingeroot
1 clove garlic, minced
¼ tsp (1 mL) salt
⅛ tsp (0.5 mL) white pepper
6 skinless salmon fillets, 5 oz. (150 g) each
Citrus Maple Glaze (recipe follows)

Preheat oven to 350°F (180°C). Combine oil, lemon juice, chili powder,
ginger, garlic, salt and pepper in a ceramic baking dish. Add salmon fillets,
turning to coat. Marinate for 5 minutes. Transfer salmon to an ovenproof
dish and bake for 8 minutes or until fish flakes easily when tested with a fork.
To serve, top each fillet with a little Citrus Maple Glaze.

Serves 6

CITRUS MAPLE GLAZE:

juice of 1 lemon
juice of 1 lime
juice of 1 orange
1 cup (250 mL) pure maple syrup
1 tbsp (15 mL) finely chopped fresh cilantro
freshly grated pepper

In a saucepan over medium heat, reduce citrus juices to consistency of
syrup. Stir in maple syrup and continue to reduce to a syrup consistency.
Let stand until cooled slightly. At serving time, stir in cilantro and season to
taste with pepper.

MANOIR VICTORIA GRILLED CHICKEN

Manoir Victoria, Quebec City, PQ

The chef suggests that his marinated chicken pieces are equally delicious cooked on a barbecue grill. He serves the chicken napped with his wonderful maple sauce.

1 chicken, 3–4 lb. (1.5–2 kg)
½ cup (125 mL) vegetable oil
¼ cup (60 mL) wine vinegar
1 tbsp (15 mL) soya sauce
1 tbsp (15 mL) finely chopped fresh ginger
2 cloves garlic, minced
¼ cup (60 mL) pure maple syrup
2 tbsp (30 mL) lemon juice

Rinse chicken and pat dry; cut into 4–6 serving pieces. Combine remaining ingredients and marinate chicken, covered and refrigerated, for up to 24 hours. Turn chicken pieces to ensure that they are covered with marinade.

Preheat oven to 400°F (200°C). Place chicken in an ovenproof dish and bake until tender, approximately 40 to 45 minutes. Baste occasionally with pan juices and reserved marinade. Serve napped with Manoir Victoria Maple Sauce (recipe follows).

Serves 4

MANOIR VICTORIA MAPLE SAUCE:

½ cup (125 mL) pure maple syrup
3 tbsp (45 mL) butter, at room temperature
1 tbsp (15 mL) soya sauce
1 clove garlic, finely chopped
salt, pepper and cayenne, to taste

While chicken is baking, combine maple syrup, butter, soya sauce and garlic in a small saucepan and bring to a boil. Reduce heat and simmer until sauce is reduced by half and thickened. Season to taste with salt, pepper and cayenne.

Yields ⅓ cup (75 mL) sauce

MAPLE BALSAMIC GLAZED SALMON WITH WARM PARSNIP PURÉE

Restaurant Les Fougères, Chelsea, PQ

Balsamic vinegar is like wine—you get what you pay for, and with that being said, I suggest you buy the finest quality balsamic vinegar that your budget will accommodate.

1 cup (250 mL) pure maple syrup
1 cup (250 mL) good quality balsamic vinegar
6 Atlantic salmon fillets, 5–6 oz. (140–170 g) each
all-purpose flour seasoned with salt and pepper, for dredging
1 tbsp (15 mL) vegetable oil
1 tbsp (15 mL) butter
Warm Parsnip Purée (recipe follows)

In a saucepan over medium heat, bring maple syrup and vinegar to a boil. Lower heat and simmer until reduced by one-half and thickened to a syrupy consistency. Set glaze aside and keep warm.

Roll salmon lightly in seasoned flour. Heat oil and butter over medium-high heat and brown salmon on both sides, then transfer to 375°F (190°C) oven for 8 minutes.

To serve, brush top of salmon with maple balsamic glaze and serve on a mound of Warm Parsnip Purée. Garnish with an extra drizzle of glaze.

Serves 6

WARM PARSNIP PURÉE:

2 lb. (1 kg) parsnips, peeled and chopped
½ cup (125 mL) butter
¼ cup (60 mL) heavy cream (35% m.f.)
¼ cup (60 mL) sherry
zest of half an orange
freshly grated nutmeg, salt and pepper, to taste

Cover parsnips with cold water and bring to a boil. Reduce heat and simmer until tender. Drain and process until very smooth. Stir in remaining ingredients and process to combine.

MAPLE-ROASTED SALMON WITH MAPLE BOURBON SAUCE

Horizons Restaurant, Burnaby, BC

Ever proud of West Coast cuisine, the chef at Horizons Restaurant serves his succulent salmon accompanied by skewers of shrimp and a colourful array of crisp vegetables.

1 cup (250 mL) pure maple syrup
1 cup (250 mL) freshly squeezed
   orange juice
2 tbsp (30 mL) freshly squeezed
   lemon juice
1 tbsp (15 mL) ground black pepper
2 tbsp (30 mL) liquid honey
6 salmon fillets, 7 oz. (200 g) each
2 tbsp (30 mL) clarified butter
Maple Bourbon Sauce (recipe follows)

In a shallow dish, combine maple syrup, orange juice, lemon juice, black pepper and honey. Marinate salmon fillets, refrigerated, in the syrup mixture for at least 6 hours or overnight.

Preheat oven to 400°F (200°C). Heat the clarified butter in a large ovenproof skillet and sear the salmon fillets for about 1 minute. Turn fillets and transfer skillet to oven and bake until fish is firm to the touch, about 8 minutes. Serve immediately on a bed of Maple Bourbon Sauce.

Serves 6

MAPLE BOURBON SAUCE:

¾ cup (175 mL) chicken stock
½ cup (125 mL) dry white wine
½ cup (125 mL) heavy cream (35% m.f.)
⅓ cup (75 mL) pure maple syrup
2 tsp (10 mL) bourbon (e.g., Jack
   Daniel's or Wild Turkey)

Combine chicken stock and white wine in a small pot over high heat; bring to a boil and reduce by one-half. Lower heat to medium and whisk in heavy cream. Return to a boil and reduce again by one-third.

Stir in maple syrup and return to a boil. Immediately lower heat and simmer 20 minutes, stirring occasionally. Remove from heat and let stand 5 minutes. Whisk in bourbon. Serve warm.

Yields 1 cup (250 mL) sauce

MAPLE-BOURBON GLAZED SHRIMP

Smith Restaurant at Inn at the Forks, Winnipeg, MN

Executive chef Barry Saunders serves this dish accompanied by rice pilaf or pasta and a green salad. He notes that the flambé aspect of the preparation is always a crowd-pleaser.

2 tbsp (30 mL) vegetable oil
12 oz. (340 g) raw black tiger shrimp, peeled and deveined (16–20 size)
¼ cup (60 mL) bourbon (e.g., Jack Daniel's or Wild Turkey)
2 tbsp (30 mL) unsalted butter
2 tbsp (30 mL) pure maple syrup
fine sea salt and pepper, to taste
1 tbsp (15 mL) chopped chives
fresh lemon wedges, for garnish

Preheat oil in a skillet over medium-high heat; add shrimp and cook about 2 minutes per side, or until shrimp begin turn pink. Carefully add bourbon and ignite. When all the alcohol has burned off reduce heat; stir in butter and maple syrup.

Cook until butter is incorporated with the liquid in the pan. Season to taste with salt and pepper. Spoon over rice or pasta; garnish with a sprinkling of chives and lemon wedges.

Serves 2

MAPLE CHICKEN

Chateau Beauvallon, Mt. Tremblant, PQ

The innkeepers at Chateau Beauvallon serve traditional French Canadian dishes using local ingredients. I feel their Maple Chicken reflects the best of Québécois cuisine.

1 chicken, 3½–4 lb. (1.75–2 kg)
salt and pepper, to taste
1 tbsp (15 mL) vegetable oil
2 tbsp (30 mL) diced celery
2 tbsp (30 mL) diced carrot
1½ tbsp (22 mL) minced leek, white
   part only

¼ cup (60 mL) pure maple syrup
⅓ cup (75 mL) cider vinegar
1 cup (250 mL) chicken stock
1½ tbsp (22 mL) pure maple syrup
   (second amount)
1 tbsp (15 mL) butter, softened
1 tbsp (15 mL) all-purpose flour

Preheat oven to 450°F (230°C). Rinse chicken and pat dry; season cavity with salt and pepper and rub skin with oil. Roast, breast side up, in an open roasting pan for 10 minutes. Reduce heat to 350°F (180°C) and continue to bake the bird for about 30 minutes.

Add celery, carrot, leek and ¼ cup (60 mL) maple syrup to pan juices. Baste the bird and continue to bake another 30 minutes. Stir in vinegar and baste bird again. Continue to bake and baste until bird is tender and a thermometer inserted into the thickest part of the thigh, not touching bone, reaches an internal temperature of 185°F (85°C). Remove chicken to a heated platter and tent with foil.

Place roasting pan over medium heat and stir in chicken stock and 1½ tablespoons (22 mL) maple syrup; bring to a simmer. Cream together the butter and flour to form beurre manie and add to sauce, stirring until lightly thickened. Strain sauce.

Brush chicken with a little sauce, return to a 500°F (240°C) oven and glaze several minutes. Serve remaining sauce in a separate bowl at tableside.

Serves 4

LAKE BROME DUCKLING BRAISED IN MAPLE SYRUP SAUCE

Aux Anciens Canadiens, Quebec City, PQ

The chef at Aux Anciens Canadiens debones the duck cutlets and removes all skin, thus eliminating much of the grease that normally accompanies the meat. Serve the cutlets accompanied by rice and seasonal vegetables.

4 duck cutlets, deboned and skin removed
vegetable oil for browning
Maple Syrup Sauce (recipe follows)

Preheat oven to 350°F (180°C). Prepare duck cutlets and sear in a lightly greased skillet, turning once. Remove duck to an ovenproof baking dish and roast for approximately 10 minutes or until duck is lightly pink in the centre. Serve napped with Maple Syrup Sauce.

Serves 4

MAPLE SYRUP SAUCE:

The chef at Aux Anciens Canadiens prepares demi-glace in the classic manner by reducing stock, maple syrup and lemon zest. For the ease of the home cook, I am supplying a simplified version.

1 package Knorr demi-glace
¾ cup (175 mL) cold water
½ cup (125 mL) pure maple syrup
1 tsp (5 mL) chocolate syrup
½ tsp (2 mL) lemon zest, blanched

In a saucepan stir demi-glace mix with cold water and maple syrup. Bring to a boil over medium-high heat, stirring frequently with a whisk. Add chocolate syrup and lemon zest, reduce heat and simmer 3 minutes, stirring occasionally. Strain and serve.

ALGONQUIN MAPLE AND MUSTARD BARBECUED LAMB CHOPS

The Algonquin Resort, Saint Andrews, NB

We suggest you prepare the marinade a day in advance to allow the flavours to blend. You may experiment by adding more garlic and ginger for a stronger flavour or chopped chilli pepper for spice! While in this presentation, it is served with grilled lamb chops, the chefs suggest it is a multi-purpose marinade and will also complement chicken, pork or beef.

½ cup (125 mL) pure maple syrup
1 tbsp (15 mL) Dijon-style grainy mustard
grated zest and juice of 1 fresh lemon
4 tsp (20 mL) balsamic vinegar
4–6 twists of freshly grated pepper
1 garlic clove, finely chopped
1 tsp (5 mL) finely grated fresh ginger
¼ cup (60 mL) canola oil
12 rib lamb chops, 2–3 oz. (60–90 g) each

Blend together all ingredients except the lamb chops. Refrigerate, covered, for 24 hours.

Marinate the meat, refrigerated, for 45 minutes, then barbecue over low to medium heat until meat is browned on the outside and pink on the inside. Brush with marinade while grilling to keep meat moist.

Serves 4

Falcourt Inn's Maple Meringues with Peaches, p. 68

DESSERTS

There are two types of cookbook fanatics. The first looks over the main course selections and the second rushes to the desserts. If sweets are your thing, then the maple syrup desserts that follow are all you will ever need to complete your dinner.

FALCOURT INN'S MAPLE MERINGUES WITH PEACHES

Falcourt Inn, Nictaux, NS

Meringues will keep for up to a week if stored in an airtight container. They are easy to prepare and are the basis of many stunning desserts.

4 egg whites, at room temperature
pinch of salt
¼ tsp (1 mL) cream of tartar
¼ cup (60 mL) pure maple syrup
drop of vanilla
¼ cup (60 mL) pure maple syrup (second amount)
16 fresh or canned peach slices
mint leaves, as garnish

Preheat oven to 250°F (120°C). In a large bowl, beat egg whites, salt and cream of tartar until soft peaks form. Slowly add ¼ cup (60 mL) maple syrup and vanilla and continue to beat until stiff glossy peaks form. Pipe or spoon onto a baking sheet lined with parchment paper, forming small rounds. Place in oven and bake approximately 1 hour; turn off heat and leave meringues in oven until cooled to room temperature. Remove and store in an airtight container up to 1 week.

Yields 10–12 meringues

Marinate peach slices in ¼ cup (60 mL) maple syrup for at least one hour. To serve, place meringue in centre of dessert plate; surround with peach slices. Garnish with mint leaves.

Serves 4–6

PARKER'S LODGE MAPLE SYRUP SQUARES

The Parker's Lodge, Val-David, PQ

Guaranteed to satisfy the most discriminating sweet tooth, these squares are easy to prepare and oh, so delicious.

BASE:
½ cup (125 mL) butter at room temperature
¼ cup (60 mL) brown sugar
1 cup (250 mL) all-purpose flour

TOPPING:
⅔ cup (150 mL) brown sugar, firmly packed
2 eggs, beaten
¼ tsp (1 mL) salt
1 cup (250 mL) walnuts or pecans, chopped
1 cup (250 mL) pure maple syrup
2 tbsp (30 mL) all-purpose flour
1 tsp (5 mL) vanilla

Preheat oven to 350°F (180°C). Using a mixer, combine butter, brown sugar and flour and mix well. Press into a greased and floured 8 inch (20 cm) square baking pan; bake 15 minutes.

In a large bowl combine topping ingredients and pour over base. Return to oven and bake an additional 30 minutes or until topping is browned and bubbly. Cool and cut into squares

Serves 16

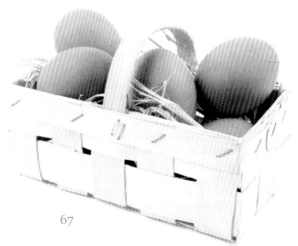

DUNDEE MAPLE BUTTER TARTS WITH MARITIME MAPLE SAUCE

The Dundee Arms, Charlottetown, PE

Maple flavour at its best; at the Dundee Arms, the chef decorates his plate using a real maple leaf for a spectacular presentation.

PASTRY:
1¼ cups (310 mL) all-purpose flour
pinch of salt
½ cup (125 mL) butter
2–3 tbsp (30–45 mL) ice water to bind

FILLING:
⅓ cup (75 mL) butter
⅓ cup (75 mL) pure maple syrup
½ tsp (2 mL) vanilla
1 cup (250 mL) brown sugar
pinch of salt
2 eggs

SAUCE:
2 egg yolks
⅔ cup (150 mL) pure maple syrup
¼ cup (60 mL) brown sugar
½ cup (125 mL) heavy cream (35% m.f.), whipped
¼ cup (60 mL) heavy cream (35% m.f.), unwhipped

Combine flour and salt in a mixing bowl. Cut in butter with a pastry blender until mixture is the size of large peas. Do not over-mix. Sprinkle ice water over mixture and blend with a fork until absorbed. Form into a ball and roll out on a floured surface. Cut into eight 3½ inch (9 cm) rounds and place in muffin tins. Set aside.

Preheat oven to 375°F (190°C). To prepare filling, melt butter in a saucepan over medium heat. Add syrup, vanilla, brown sugar and salt; mix well. Beat eggs in a separate bowl and add to mixture. Fill pastries and bake approximately 15 minutes, until tarts are browned and filling is bubbly. Remove from oven and set aside 10 minutes.

While pastries are baking, prepare sauce. In a double boiler, over simmering but not boiling water, heat egg yolks, maple syrup and brown sugar until mixture thickens and coats the back of a spoon. Cool over ice cubes, stirring constantly. Fold in whipped cream, then fold in unwhipped cream. Refrigerate.

To serve, spread a little sauce on a dessert plate and top with tart.

Serves 8

PECAN AND MAPLE SYRUP PUDDING

Muskoka Grandview Inn, Huntsville, ON

The chef at Muskoka Grandview Inn suggests serving this delectable pudding with ice cream or whipped cream, garnished with fresh summer berries and mint.

1 cup (250 mL) unsalted butter, softened
1 cup (250 mL) granulated sugar
4 eggs
1 tsp (5 mL) vanilla
3 cups (750 mL) all-purpose flour, sifted
1 cup (250 mL) chopped pecans (divided)
2 tbsp (30 mL) baking powder
½ tsp (2 mL) cinnamon
grated zest of 1 lemon
¾ cup (175 mL) milk
1 cup (250 mL) pure maple syrup (divided)

Preheat oven to 350°F (180°C). In a large bowl, beat together butter and sugar until creamy. Gradually beat in the eggs and vanilla. In a separate bowl, combine flour, ¾ cup (175 mL) pecans, baking powder, cinnamon and lemon zest. Gradually fold into butter mixture, alternating with milk, until batter is smooth.

Lightly grease a 10 cup (2.5 L) pudding mold or ovenproof bowl with vegetable spray or oil, and line the bottom with a circle of parchment or waxed paper. Pour ¾ cup (175 mL) maple syrup into mold and sprinkle with remaining pecans. Pour in batter and top with remaining maple syrup. Cover mold with foil and place in a large baking dish or roasting pan; pour in enough water to come halfway up the side of the mold. Bake 2 hours or until a tester inserted in the centre comes out clean. Unmold onto serving platter.

Serves 6–8

LISCOMBE LODGE MAPLE SYRUP CREAM

Liscombe Lodge, Liscomb Mills, NS

This simple, elegant dessert makes a beautiful presentation served in stemmed glasses, decorated with fresh seasonal berries and mint leaves.

1 tbsp (15 mL) powdered gelatin
¼ cup (60 mL) cold water
½ cup (125 mL) milk, scalded
⅔ cup (150 mL) pure maple syrup
⅛ tsp (0.5 mL) salt
2 cups (500 mL) heavy cream (35% m.f.), whipped
fresh fruit and mint leaves as garnish

Soak gelatin in cold water for 5 minutes, then stir into scalded milk. Add maple syrup and salt and chill until mixture begins to thicken, about 45 minutes. Prepare whipped cream and gently fold into gelatin mixture. Pour into a large bowl or six individual serving dishes. Chill several hours until firm. Serve garnished with fruit and mint leaves, if desired.

Serves 6

"GRAND-PERES" AU SIROP D'ERABLE

The Parker's Lodge, Val-David, PQ

Hmmm—a dumpling with a difference. This is a simple-to-prepare dessert, but oh, so good. Chef Rollande Thisdele at the Parker's Lodge serves this dessert warm from the oven in individual serving dishes with a generous dollop of whipped cream.

1 cup (250 mL) pure maple syrup
1 cup (250 mL) water
1 cup (250 mL) all-purpose flour
½ tsp (2 mL) salt
2 tsp (10 mL) baking powder
1 tbsp (15 mL) butter
½ cup (125 mL) milk
½ cup (125 mL) heavy cream (35% m.f.), whipped

In a deep pot, bring maple syrup and water to a boil. In a bowl, whisk together flour, salt, and baking powder. Cut in butter with a pastry blender and stir in milk to make a soft dough. Drop the batter by spoonfuls on top of the simmering maple sauce. Immediately cover saucepan and cook over medium heat without removing cover for 15 to 18 minutes. Serve warm with sauce and a dollop of whipped cream.

Serves 4–6

MAPLE MOUSSE WITH STRAWBERRY AND RHUBARB COMPOTE

The Norsemen Restaurant and Walker Lake Resort, Huntsville, ON

This dessert is worth every last calorie—the silky-smooth mousse combined with the colourful tart compote is heavenly.

4 egg yolks
1 cup (250 mL) pure maple syrup
2 tbsp (30 mL) bourbon or rum
1 tsp (5 mL) powdered gelatin
1 tbsp (15 ml) warm water
1 cup (250 mL) heavy cream (35% m.f.)
Strawberry and Rhubarb Compote (recipe follows)

In the top of a double boiler over simmering water, whisk together egg yolks and maple syrup; blend in bourbon. Cook, whisking constantly, until soft peaks form. Remove from heat. Dissolve gelatin in water and add to maple mixture, whisking to incorporate. Let cool but do not allow to set.

Whip cream until stiff peaks form. Using a rubber spatula, fold into the cooled maple mixture. Spoon into four to six ramekins and refrigerate 2 to 3 hours or until set. To serve, place a spoonful of compote in the centre of each serving plate and top with mousse.

Serves 4–6

STRAWBERRY AND RHUBARB COMPOTE:

1 pint (500 mL) fresh strawberries, rinsed, hulled and coarsely chopped
3 stalks rhubarb, coarsely chopped
¾ cup (175 mL) icing sugar
1½ tbsp (22 mL) freshly squeezed lemon juice
½ cup (125 mL) fresh blueberries

In a saucepan over medium-low heat, combine chopped strawberries, rhubarb, icing sugar and lemon juice; simmer until rhubarb is soft. Stir in blueberries and simmer 2 minutes, being careful to keep blueberries whole. Transfer to a bowl, cover and refrigerate until chilled.

ACADIAN APPLE PIE

Delta Beausejour Hotel, Moncton, NB

The Windjammer Dining Room of Moncton's Delta Beausejour has been the "go to" restaurant for special occasions. Their decadent Acadian Apple Pie is but one example of why Monctonians love The Beau.

½ cup (125 mL) raisins
¾ cup (175 mL) apple juice
⅓ cup (75 mL) water
½ cup (125 mL) granulated sugar
4 medium-large apples, peeled and sliced
¼ tsp (1 mL) salt
1 tsp (5 mL) grated lemon zest
½ tsp (2 mL) lemon juice
1 tbsp (15 mL) butter
¼ tsp (1 mL) cinnamon
2 tbsp (30 mL) cornstarch
⅓ cup (75 mL) cold water
¾ cup (175 mL) walnut pieces
9 inch (23 cm) pie plate lined with
  Sweet Dough (recipe follows)
¼ cup (60 mL) melted butter
½ cup (125 mL) granulated sugar
½ cup (125 mL) all-purpose flour
½ cup (125 mL) rolled oats
¼ cup (60 mL) pure maple syrup
  for topping

Rinse and dry raisins. In a saucepan, combine raisins, apple juice, water, ½ cup (125 mL) sugar, apples, salt, lemon zest and juice, 1 tbsp (15 mL) butter, and cinnamon. Bring to a boil, reduce heat and simmer over medium heat for 5 minutes. Dissolve cornstarch in ⅓ cup (75 mL) cold water and stir into raisin mixture. Bring to a boil, then simmer three minutes. Remove from heat and stir in walnuts. Spoon mixture into prepared pie plate that has been lined with Sweet Dough.

Preheat oven to 350°F (180°C). Mix together melted butter, ½ cup (125 mL) sugar, flour and oats and sprinkle over pie. Bake 35 to 45 minutes until lightly browned. Serve warm or chilled, drizzled with maple syrup.

Serves 6–8

SWEET DOUGH:

⅓ cup (75 mL) granulated sugar
⅓ cup (75 mL) butter, softened
1 small egg, beaten
1 cup (250 mL) all-purpose flour

With a mixer, whip sugar and butter until light and fluffy. Add egg and continue to beat. Mix in flour and form into a ball. Roll the dough on a floured surface to fit into a shallow 9 inch (23 cm) pie plate.

MAPLE SABAYON ON MARINATED BERRIES

Harvest Dining Room, Fairmont Hotel MacDonald, Edmonton, AB

The choice of berries in this recipe depends upon the season, but be assured you will receive raves however you serve it.

4 cups (1 L) seasonal berries (strawberries, raspberries, blueberries, etc.)
½ cup (125 mL) Grand Marnier liqueur
3 egg yolks
¼ cup (60 mL) granulated sugar
¼ cup (60 mL) pure maple syrup
¼ cup (60 mL) white wine
mint leaves, as garnish

Place berries in a bowl and drizzle with Grand Marnier. Spoon into 4 heatproof bowls and set aside.

Whisk egg yolks and sugar in a heatproof bowl until foamy and pale. Set bowl over a pan of simmering water. Whisk constantly, adding maple syrup and wine, a little at a time, until the mixture is fluffy and thickened.

Preheat broiler. Spoon sauce over berries and brown under a broiler until golden, 1 to 2 minutes. Serve immediately, garnished with mint leaves.

Serves 4

MARBLE GREEN APPLE AND MAPLE SYRUP CHEESECAKE WITH CARAMEL SAUCE

The Inn at Manitou, McKellar, ON

For an autumn version of this amazing cheesecake, the chef suggests replacing the applesauce with pumpkin purée and omitting the food colouring.

CRUST:

1 cup (250 mL) all-purpose flour
¾ tsp (4 mL) cinnamon
¾ tsp (4 mL) baking powder
¼ tsp (1 mL) freshly grated nutmeg
¼ tsp (1 mL) ground ginger
¼ tsp (1 mL) salt
¼ tsp (1 mL) ground cloves
¼ tsp (1 mL) salt
4 tbsp (60 mL) butter, softened
2 tbsp (30 mL) granulated sugar
1 large egg yolk
1½ tbsp (22 mL) pure maple syrup

Sift together flour, spices and salt in a bowl. In a separate bowl, beat together butter and sugar until light and fluffy, about 3 minutes. Blend in egg yolk and maple syrup. Mix into dry ingredients, cover and refrigerate 2 to 3 hours.

Preheat oven to 350°F (180°C). Press crust mixture into bottom of lightly greased 9 inch (23 cm) springform pan and bake 10 to 15 minutes or until lightly browned. Remove from oven and cool.

CHEESECAKE FILLING:

12 oz. (375 g) cream cheese, softened
⅔ cup (150 mL) granulated sugar
1½ tbsp (22 mL) pure maple syrup
1 drop green food colouring
¾ cup (175 mL) heavy cream (35% m.f.)
½ cup (125 mL) sour cream
1 large egg
1 large egg yolk
2 tsp (10 mL) lime juice
1½ cup (375 mL) unsweetened
  applesauce
1 tsp (5 mL) cinnamon
½ tsp (2 mL) ground ginger
½ tsp (2 mL) ground cloves
10 to 12 fresh mint sprigs, as garnish
Caramel Sauce (recipe follows)

Preheat oven to 300°F (150°C). In a large bowl beat together cream cheese, sugar, maple syrup and food colouring until smooth. Add cream, sour cream, egg, egg yolk and lime juice; beat at medium speed until combined. Transfer half of the batter to a separate bowl and set aside.

To the remaining batter, add applesauce, cinnamon, ginger and cloves and beat until combined. Pour over crust. Pour plain batter over top and run a knife through batter just enough to create a marble effect. Bake 30 to 45 minutes or until set. Let cool. Run a wet, hot knife around the edge of the springform pan; remove side.

Slice cheesecake just before serving. Spoon Caramel Sauce over top and garnish with mint sprigs.

Serves 10–12

CARAMEL SAUCE:

1 cup (250 mL) granulated sugar
2 cups (500 mL) heavy cream (35% m.f.)

Melt sugar in a saucepan over low heat, stirring constantly until light brown. Gradually pour in cream, stirring until all sugar is dissolved and sauce is heated through. Pour sauce through a sieve into a bowl. Cover and refrigerate.

BLUEBERRY MAPLE CHIFFON CONES

We suggest preparing the cones and maple chiffon early in the day. The batter tends to spread, so you should allow only 3 or 4 cones per baking sheet. Serve garnished with fresh berries of the season.

TULIP CONES:

7 tbsp (105 mL) butter, softened
1 cup (250 mL) icing sugar
7 tbsp (105 mL) egg whites
½ cup (125 mL) flour

Preheat oven to 350°F (180°C). With an electric mixer, combine butter, icing sugar, egg whites and flour. Line two baking sheets with foil and liberally spray with no-stick cooking spray. Allowing approximately 2 tbsp (30 mL) of dough per cone, spread out on the foil in a circle and bake only until the dough is brown on the edges. Remove from oven and quickly shape into cones, using metal cream horn molds if available; allow to cool.

MAPLE CHIFFON:

4 eggs
½ cup (125 mL) pure maple syrup
½ cup (125 mL) granulated sugar
1 tbsp (15 mL) lemon juice
1 tbsp (15 mL) powdered gelatin
¼ cup (60 mL) hot water
2 cups (500 mL) heavy cream (35% m.f.), whipped
½–¾ cup (125–175 mL) fresh blueberries
additional maple syrup for garnish

In the top half of a double boiler, over medium heat, whisk together eggs, maple syrup, sugar and lemon juice until thick and frothy and sugar is dissolved. Combine gelatin and hot water and whisk into egg syrup mixture.

Remove from heat and whisk over ice cubes until cool. Fold in whipped cream and refrigerate several hours.

To serve, pipe maple chiffon into cones, garnish with fresh blueberries and a drizzle of maple syrup.

Serves 4–6

PECAN AND MAPLE SYRUP TART

Bishops Restaurant, Vancouver, BC

This version of a southern classic, made Canadian with the addition of maple syrup, is neither too sweet nor too runny, as can be sometimes the case with a pecan pie. Executive chef Dennis Green suggests making the pie a day in advance as the filling benefits from time in the refrigerator to help it set firmly.

PASTRY:

¾ cup (175 mL) all-purpose flour
1 tsp (5 mL) sugar
½ tsp (2 mL) salt
6 tbsp (90 mL) butter, softened
1–1½ tbsp (15–22 mL) cold water

Preheat oven to 350°F (180°C). Combine flour, sugar and salt in a bowl. Add butter and mix until the texture becomes coarse and mealy. Sprinkle with water and combine well. Mix until dough forms a ball, taking care not to over-mix.

On a lightly floured surface, roll out pastry to form a round 12 inches (30 cm) in diameter. Line a 10 inch (25 cm) tart pan with the pastry and use the back of the tines of a fork to press down around the edge. Line the bottom of the pastry with a piece of parchment paper and fill with dried beans or pastry weights. Bake until pastry just begins to colour around the edges, about 20 minutes. Remove the dried beans and allow the pie shell to cool.

FILLING:

2 cups (500 mL) whole pecans, lightly toasted
1 cup (250 mL) granulated sugar
2 tbsp (30 mL) all-purpose flour
1 cup (250 mL) pure maple syrup
3 eggs
2 tsp (10 mL) vanilla
whipped cream, as garnish

Preheat oven to 300°F (150°C). Spread pecans evenly over a baking sheet and toast 3 to 5 minutes. Remove from oven and set aside to cool; arrange pecans evenly over the bottom of the pastry shell.

Whisk together the sugar, flour, maple syrup, eggs and vanilla in a bowl. Pour gently over pecans.

Preheat oven to 350°F (180°C) and bake pie until slightly puffed and centre wiggles slightly when the pan is tapped, about 35 to 45 minutes. Allow to cool completely, then cover and chill thoroughly in the refrigerator before serving. Garnish pie with whipped cream.

Serves 6–8

MAPLE MOUSSE

The Parker's Lodge, Val-David, PQ

This dessert recipe is a bit lighter than most in this collection and we are sure it will become a family favourite.

2 tbsp powdered gelatin
½ cup (125 mL) cold water
1 cup (250 mL) boiling water
1½ cups (375 mL) pure maple syrup
2 egg whites
½ cup (125 mL) chopped walnuts or almonds

Soak gelatin in cold water for 5 minutes to soften. Add boiling water and stir until gelatin is completely dissolved. Stir in maple syrup and refrigerate until it resembles the consistency of egg whites. Remove from refrigerator and whip with an electric mixer. In a separate bowl, whip egg whites until stiff. Gently fold egg whites and nuts into gelatin mixture and turn out into a decorative serving bowl. Refrigerate until set.

Serves 8

MAPLE SYRUP PIE

Aux Anciens Canadiens, Quebec City, PQ

Located in the heart of old Quebec City, the Aux Anciens Canadiens serves this traditional pie accompanied by a spoonful of whipped cream.

1½ cups (375 mL) brown sugar
½ cup (125 mL) heavy cream (35% m.f.)
⅓ cup (75 mL) pure maple syrup
1 large egg, at room temperature
2 tsp (10 mL) butter, at room temperature
an 8 inch (20 cm) prebaked pie shell
whipped cream, as garnish

Preheat oven to 350°F (180°C). In a large bowl with an electric mixer, blend together brown sugar, cream, maple syrup, egg and butter until smooth and creamy. Pour into prepared pie shell and bake 45 minutes. Remove from oven and cool to room temperature. Serve garnished with freshly whipped cream.

Serves 6

TARTE AU FONDANT À L'ÉRABLE

Chateau Bonne Entente, Sainte Foy, PQ

Quebec pure maple syrup is an intrinsic ingredient at the restaurant of Chateau Bonne Entente. I'm sure after you try this delicious pie, the recipe will become a family favourite.

2 cups (500 mL) graham cracker crumbs
⅓ cup (75 mL) pure maple syrup
⅓ cup (75 mL) butter, melted
¼ cup (60 mL) butter (second amount)
1 cup (250 mL) caramels, preferably maple-flavoured (30–32)
1 cup (250 mL) 2% milk, warmed
3 large egg yolks
1 envelope unflavoured gelatin
3 tbsp (45 mL) cold water
¼ cup (60 mL) boiling water
Fresh fruit and icing sugar, as garnish

Preheat oven to 375°F (190°C). Prepare crust by mixing together graham cracker crumbs, ⅓ cup (75 mL) maple syrup and melted butter. Pat into a lightly greased 9 inch (23 cm) pie plate and bake 8 minutes. Remove from oven and set aside to cool.

Over boiling water in a double boiler, combine second amount of butter, caramels and warm milk. Cook, stirring constantly, until caramels are melted and mixture comes to a boil. Remove from stove and immediately whisk in egg yolks, stirring until fully incorporated. Sprinkle gelatin over cold water and allow to soften, about 5 minutes. Stir boiling water into gelatin, then fold into caramel mixture. Pour into prepared crust, cover with plastic wrap and refrigerate until firm, about 3 to 4 hours.

At serving time, slice pie in wedges and garnish with fresh fruit and a sprinkle of icing sugar.

Serves 6–8

CREAMY MAPLE FONDUE

Ste. Anne's Country Inn and Spa, Grafton, ON

The chef at Ste. Anne's Country Inn and Spa suggests, as a delicious alternative, that you use crème fraiche in place of the cream.

½ cup (125 mL) pure maple syrup
2 tsp (10 mL) cornstarch
2½ cups (625 mL) light cream (18% m.f.), divided
assorted firm fruits and berries, cut into small pieces

Gently heat maple syrup in a saucepan for 5 minutes. In a bowl combine cornstarch with 2 tsp (10 mL) of the cream. Bring the remaining cream to a boil in a separate saucepan, then stir into maple syrup. Stir cornstarch mixture into syrup mixture and heat gently, stirring continuously until thickened. To serve, keep sauce warm in a fondue pot or ceramic dish placed over a spirit lamp. Using fondue forks, dip fruit into sauce.

Serves 4–6

COFFEE AND MAPLE CHARLOTTE

Ste. Anne's Country Inn and Spa, Grafton, ON

Soft silken tofu is found in the dairy section of most supermarkets. At Ste. Anne's Country Inn and Spa, the chef incorporates tofu into his charlotte, thus accommodating his health-conscious guests.

4 tsp (20 mL) powdered gelatin
¼ cup (60 mL) cold water
1 cup (250 mL) pure maple syrup
12 oz. (300 g) soft silken tofu
1 package lady fingers
½ cup (125 mL) cold coffee
¼ cup (60 mL) pure maple syrup (second amount)
fresh fruit, as garnish

Sprinkle gelatin over cold water and allow to stand 5 minutes. Using a double boiler, melt gelatin over simmering water until clear. Stir in 1 cup (250 mL) maple syrup and return to a boil; remove from heat and cool.

Using a food processor, pulse tofu until smooth. Slowly add cooled maple syrup mixture and pulse to incorporate. Scrape down the sides of the food processor bowl with a rubber spatula and mix until smooth.

Line a 9 inch (23 cm) dish with lady fingers. Combine coffee and ¼ cup (60 mL) maple syrup and drizzle over lady fingers. Pour tofu mixture over and chill for a minimum of 3 hours. Serve in squares with fresh fruit on the side.

Serves 6–8

MAPLE PARFAIT

For many years, The Palliser Restaurant was a landmark in Truro, Nova Scotia, and the owner relayed the story that as a child, she refused to eat Christmas pudding. Her mother developed this recipe and served it only for the holidays, thus they affectionately called it "Maple Christmas" Parfait.

½ cup (125 mL) pure maple syrup
2 eggs, at room temperature
1 cup (250 mL) heavy cream (35% m.f.)
creme de cacao, whipped cream and chocolate sprinkles for garnish

In a small saucepan heat maple syrup almost to a boil. Remove from heat and place in a mixing bowl. Add eggs and beat on medium-high speed until mixture is fully blended, approximately 5 minutes. Refrigerate several hours or overnight until well chilled.

Whip heavy cream until stiff peaks form, then, using an electric mixer, beat into maple mixture. Pour into parfait glasses, cover with plastic wrap and freeze. Remove from freezer 10 minutes before serving. Garnish with a teaspoon of crème de cacao, dollop of whipped cream and chocolate sprinkles.

Serves 6–8

INDEX

PHOTO CREDITS